Look out for dragons!

Keith Gaines

The old man and the dragons of Norton

'Is everybody ready?' said Kevin.

'I'm ready,' said William. 'I have two big bottles of fizzy drink.'

'I'm ready,' said Robert. 'I have three cakes.'

'And I have our sandwiches,' said Kevin, 'so let's get on our bikes and go to the woods for our picnic.'

The three friends lived about a mile away from the woods and they went there often.

'I'm a bit worried about the weather,' said Kevin. 'It was raining earlier. It may rain when we have our picnic.'

'But the sun's coming out now,' said William.

'Look over there,' shouted Robert. 'It's a rainbow. And the end of the rainbow is in the woods.'

'No it's not,' laughed Kevin. 'You can't get to the end of a rainbow.'

The three friends cycled towards the woods.

'What shall we do when we get there?' said William.

'Let's explore the woods first,' said Kevin, 'then eat our picnic later.'

'No, let's eat our picnic first,' said Robert. 'I'm starving!'

رحلة الأصدقاء الثلاثة

The three friends reached the edge of the woods. They rode along a narrow path through the trees.

'Let's stop here,' said Kevin after a few minutes. 'This is a nice place for a picnic.'

The three friends unpacked their sandwiches, cakes and drinks and started their picnic.

'That's funny,' said Robert, as he finished his drink.

'What's funny?' said William.

'I can still see the rainbow,' said Robert. 'And it looks much closer now. It's just behind those trees over there.'

'Perhaps we should have a look,' said Kevin. 'Let's put away our picnic things.'

4

The three friends pushed their bikes through the trees.

'Look, the rainbow looks really close now,' said William.

'That's very unusual,' said Kevin.

'Wow!' exclaimed Robert.

They were in a small round clearing in the trees. There in front of them, shining with lots of different colours, was the rainbow.

'I don't believe it!' said Kevin. 'It's the end of the rainbow!'

The three children left their bikes by the trees and walked slowly towards the rainbow.

Robert reached out to touch the rainbow.

'Be careful!' shouted Kevin. 'You might get an electric shock or something!'

'Rainbows aren't electric!' said Robert, and he put his hand out into the rainbow.

'Well?' said Kevin.

'Nothing,' said Robert. 'There's nothing there. It's just a sort of light.'

And he walked straight through the rainbow.

'Where are you?' shouted William. 'We can't see you any more.'

'I'm here,' shouted Robert. 'I'm on the other side of the rainbow. Come and join me. It's quite safe.'

The two boys walked through the rainbow.

Now the three friends were all on the other side of the rainbow.

'It looks different on this side,' said Robert.

'What do you mean?' asked William.

'I don't know,' said Robert. 'It's darker and – more frightening. And I have a funny feeling that we are not alone.'

'You're silly,' said William. 'It's still the same place, and we're the only people in it.'

'I'm not so sure,' said Kevin. 'Look over there!'

On the other side of the clearing, an old man with a long white beard was holding a book and stirring a pot. He was wearing long clothes.

The old man stopped stirring the pot and reached inside a little bag. He pulled something out of the bag and dropped it into the pot. Suddenly he spoke.

'Leg of frog and horn of deer,
Keep the dragons out of here.
Leaves of grass and leaves of clover,
Stop the dragons flying over.'

'What's he cooking?' said William.

'Why is he wearing a big sheet?' said Robert.

'And why is he talking to a pot?' said Kevin.

The old man looked up at the sound of their voices. He stared at the children. Then he walked over to them.

'Hello, little children,' said the old man. 'What are you doing here?'

'We're just walking through the woods,' said Kevin. 'What are you doing here?'

'I am the wise man of the woods,' replied the old man. He waved towards the pot. 'I am making a magic spell. I come here every week to make this spell.'

'What does the magic spell do?' asked Kevin.

The wise man of the woods looked around slowly and carefully. Then he leaned towards Kevin.

'My magic spell keeps the dragons away!' he whispered.

'Have you ever seen a dragon?' Kevin asked the old man.

'No, I haven't – and I don't want to,' said the wise man of the woods. 'Dragons are very dangerous. Fire comes out of their mouths, and they either burn you to ashes – or eat you!'

'Has anyone around here ever seen a dragon?' asked Kevin.

'Oh, yes!' said the wise man of the woods. 'There was a knight who lived in the castle on the other side of the woods. He wanted to show everybody that he was very brave, so one day he went out of the castle to find a dragon and bring it back.'

'And did he?' said Robert.

'No, he didn't,' said the wise man of the woods. 'Nobody ever saw him again. The dragon ate him, I'm sure of it – but he did see it before it ate him!'

'When was this?' said Kevin suspiciously.

'Oh, now, let me see – about five hundred years ago,' said the wise man of the woods, stroking his beard.

'Well, that was a very long time ago,' said Kevin. 'I don't think there are any dragons.'

The wise man of the woods looked at him closely. 'You are very young,' he said. 'Perhaps you don't know very much about the world.'

He opened his book.

'Look at this,' said the old man. 'There are lots of dragons; everybody knows that. There are great big red ones that fly and there are little green ones that walk around.'

'There aren't any dragons walking or flying around here,' said Kevin.

'Of course there aren't any dragons around here!' shouted the wise man of the woods. 'My magic spell keeps all the dragons away! That's why I make it every week. Just look around. Can you see any dragons? Of course you can't. But we mustn't talk about them so much, or they will hear us.'

'Now,' said the wise man of the woods, 'tell me about you. Who are you?'

'I'm Kevin,' said Kevin. 'This is Robert and this is William. We all live in the town over there.'

'What town?' said the wise man of the woods suspiciously.

'Norton,' said William. 'Surely you know Norton. It's a big town, with schools and shops and everything.'

The wise man of the woods looked at them.

'This is very strange,' he said, stroking his beard. 'I don't know this town, but I would like to see it. Did you buy those strange clothes in Norton?'

'Our clothes aren't strange,' said Kevin. 'Everybody wears clothes like these.'

'How did you get here?' said the wise man of the woods.

'We came here on our bikes,' said Robert. 'We came out to the woods for a picnic.'

The wise man of the woods looked very puzzled.

'Bikes... picnic... I do not know these things,' he muttered.

'Then we saw this rainbow in the woods, and when we walked through it we saw you.'

'Ahh!' said the wise man of the woods. 'You came through the rainbow. That explains it.'

'Explains what?' asked Kevin.

'The rainbow is very strong magic,' said the wise man of the woods. 'It only appears in the woods once a year. When you walk through it you go backwards or forwards in time.'

'But we are in the same place,' said Robert.

'Oh yes,' said the wise man of the woods. 'You are in the same place, but in a different time.'

Slowly, the wise man of the woods walked round the three children. He looked at them closely.

'You aren't from the past,' he said. 'Perhaps you are from the future.'

Suddenly the old man ran back to his pot and put his book down beside it.

'This is exciting,' he shouted. 'I have never seen the future. I have finished my dragon spell, and the rainbow usually stays here for about an hour. We will go back through the rainbow and you can show me... What did you call it? Norton. Come on!' The old man grabbed Robert's hand.

The wise man of the woods pulled Robert quickly towards the rainbow.

'Wait for us!' shouted Kevin and William.

They went back through the rainbow, but the old man stopped straight away and pointed to their bikes.

'What are those strange things?' said the wise man of the woods.

'Those are our bikes,' said Kevin. 'We ride them.'

The old man looked puzzled.

'They are like horses,' said William, 'but they aren't alive. You have to push the pedals round.'

'You can come on mine,' said Kevin. 'Look. You sit on the seat, and I'll stand on the pedals.'

The old man climbed onto the seat.

Then Kevin got on the pedals and they started to move.

'Don't go so fast!' yelled the old man, as Robert and William cycled past them.

Ten minutes later, the three children and the old man stood outside the fast food shop on the edge of the town.

'I enjoyed that,' said the old man. He looked closely at Kevin's bike. 'This pike is a very clever thing,' he said. 'Where can I get one for myself?'

'It's not a pike, it's a bike,' said William.

'We have an old bike in the shed,' said Robert. 'Nobody uses it. You can have it if you like. We'll go to my house and get it.'

The old man was reading the menu outside the fast food shop.

'This looks interesting,' he said. 'Fish, chicken, burger – what is "burger"?'

'It's meat,' said William. 'You cook it and put it in a bun.'

'Hmm,' said the old man. 'That sounds nice. What is "fries"?'

'It's potatoes,' said Robert. 'You cut them up and fry them.'

'What is a potato?' said the old man.

'It's big and brown. It grows under the ground,' said Kevin.

'And you eat it?' said the old man, very surprised.

The wise man of the woods looked down the road. Suddenly he looked very frightened.

'Quick, little children! We must hide!' he shouted. 'A dragon is coming! It's a big red dragon and it's puffing smoke!'

The children looked down the road. A red bus was coming towards them, with a cloud of smoke behind it.

'That's not a dragon,' said Kevin. 'That's a bus. You sit in it and it takes you to different places.'

But the wise man of the woods wasn't listening. He was running very fast along the road.

The children ran after him.

'In here,' shouted Robert. 'This is my house. You can hide in here!'

The wise man of the woods and the children stood in Robert's front garden, behind the hedge.

'That was lucky,' said the old man. 'The big red dragon has gone past. He didn't see us.'

Suddenly they heard a voice.

'Hi, Robert. Who's the old man in the sheet?'

Robert's big brother was pushing his motorbike towards the road.

'Ah,' said the old man. 'A brave knight! Look at his black helmet – but where is his sword?'

'That's not a knight,' said Robert. 'That's Dave. He's my brother.'

'Oh,' said the old man. 'Hello, Dave. You have a very fat bike.'

Dave started his motorbike.

'Brrmm, brrmm, brrmm!' went the motorbike.

'Hide, little children, hide!' shouted the wise man of the woods. 'The fat bike has changed into an angry black dragon. It will eat Dave, then it will eat us!'

'That's not a dragon,' said Robert. 'It's my brother's motorbike!'

But the wise man of the woods was running to the back of the house, while Dave rode away.

'You escaped!' exclaimed the old man, as the children ran into the back garden. He turned to Robert.

'I'm very sorry about your brother,' he said. 'Did the black dragon eat him or burn him to ashes?'

'He's all right,' said Robert. 'He often rides dragons.'

'Your brother is a very powerful magician then!' said the old man.

Robert opened the door of the shed.

'Is this your house?' said the old man. 'It's very nice. How many people live here?'

'Nobody lives here,' said Robert. 'This is our garden shed. We live in there.'

Robert pointed towards his house.

'That's not a house – that's a castle!' said the old man. 'And you – surely you are a great lord!'

'It's only a house,' said Robert.

'This is very interesting,' said the old man. 'I have never seen a castle in a town before.'

'Here you are,' said Robert, and he pulled a bike out of the shed. 'It's not very good, but you can have it if you want.'

The old man looked at the old bike.

'It's wonderful,' he said. 'But I have no money here. I can only give you this gold ring.' The old man started to pull a ring off his finger.

'That's all right,' said Robert. 'You can keep your ring. We have four other bikes and nobody ever uses this one.'

'Thank you, my lord,' said the wise man of the woods, and he bowed to Robert. 'Your family is rich, your brother is brave, and you are kind.' Then he looked worried again.

'What is it?' said Kevin.

'I don't know,' said the old man. 'I can hear a strange sound.' He looked up at the sky.

'Hide, little children, hide!' shouted the wise man of the woods. 'Another dragon is coming! It is the most terrible dragon of them all. Look!'

He pointed up at the sky.

'See! It is a flying dragon. It is huge and silver!'

Kevin looked up.

'That's not a dragon,' said Kevin. 'That's an aeroplane. You sit in it and it flies to other countries.'

But the wise man of the woods was pushing the bike towards the front of Robert's house.

'Oh, no!' said Robert. 'He's going again.'

The children ran after him. The wise man of the woods was on his bike. He was riding along the road towards the woods.

The children jumped on their bikes and soon they were all back at the rainbow. It was starting to disappear.

'Thank you for showing me your time,' said the wise man of the woods. He looked hot and his face was red.

'The rainbow is disappearing and I have to go. I am not staying here in your time, because it's full of dragons.'

The old man got back on his bike.

'I have never seen so many dragons in my life,' he said. 'You should get a wise man of the woods. He can make some magic spells for you, and then the dragons will stay away. I'm going back to my time. If I stay here, a dragon will get me.'

The wise man of the woods started cycling through the rainbow, which was disappearing.

'Goodbye!' called the children.

'Thank you for the bike!' shouted the wise man of the woods, and the rainbow disappeared.

The children rode home.

'He was a nice old man,' said William.

'And he really liked that old bike,' said Robert.

'Well, I still don't agree with him,' said Kevin. 'All that rubbish about dragons. Dragons aren't real. Everybody knows that!'

The old man and the dragons of Norton – questions

1 What did the children take with them for a picnic?

2 Who walked through the rainbow first?

3 Who did they find on the other side of the rainbow?

4 What was the old man doing?

5 Why are dragons dangerous?

6 Why were there no dragons in the woods?

7 What happens when somebody walks through the rainbow?

8 How did the children take the old man into town?

9 The old man met three 'dragons'. What were they?

10 How did the old man want to pay Robert?

11 What happened to the rainbow after an hour?

12 Why did the old man want to go back to his time?

All about dragons

Have you ever seen a dragon? NO! Because there aren't any dragons. But there are lots of dragon stories. All over the world people tell stories about dangerous animals that fly through the air.

In Chinese stories, dragons breathe out mist and make the clouds. Although they can fly, they usually do not have wings. They are clever and friendly, and they often talk to people. In stories from Europe, dragons are quite different. They have huge wings and they breathe out fire. They often guard treasure of gold and jewels. They do not like people – except for dinner!

The dragon flag

Over 2000 years ago, people in Iran used a flag with a dragon on it. When the Roman army came to Iran and fought these people, the Roman generals saw the dragon flags. They liked them, so they made their own flags with dragons on. Later the Roman army invaded the country of Wales, in Britain, and they brought their dragon flags with them. The people of Wales fought the Romans many times. They liked the dragon flags too, and, in turn, they made flags with dragons on. A red dragon is still on the flag of Wales today.

Roman soldiers saw dragon flags in Iran.

The Romans took their dragon flags to Wales.

The flag of Wales today.

Dragon bones

Dinosaurs lived millions of years ago. We know about dinosaurs today from studying their bones. When people saw dinosaur bones for the first time, they were very interested, but not surprised. They thought the bones came from dragons!

Dragon teeth

One old story says that if you collect the teeth from a dragon and put them into the ground, they will grow into soldiers. The soldiers will be your own army. Of course, you have to get the teeth from a dragon first!

Dragon blood

Another old story says that if you kill a dragon and put its blood all over you, then swords and knives can't cut you!

Some ice-cream shops put raspberry juice on top of an ice-cream. In some places in England, children call this 'Dragon's blood'!

All about dragons – questions

1 Which dragons breathed out mist and made clouds?

2 What do European dragons breathe out?

3 Which soldiers brought the dragon flag to Wales?

4 What does the flag of Wales look like?

5 Which part of a dragon will grow into soldiers?

6 What happens if you put dragon's blood all over you?

7 What is the 'Dragon's blood' on top of an ice-cream?

Macmillan Education
Between Towns Road, Oxford OX4 3PP
A division of Macmillan Publishers Limited
Companies and representatives throughout the world

www.macmillan-africa.com
www.macmillan-caribbean.com
ISBN-10: 0-333-67499-5
ISBN-13: 978-0-3336-7499-4

Text © Keith Gains 1998
Design and illustration © Macmillan Publishers Limited 1998

First published 1998

Illustrated by Tony Goffe / Linda Rogers Associates
Cover illustration by Tony Goffe / Linda Rogers Associates

Printed and bound in Egypt by Zamzam Presses

2006
14 13

Egypt